Pebble™

Helpers in Our Community

We Need Auto Mechanics

by Helen Frost

Consulting Editor: Gail Saunders-Smith, PhD

Capstone
press
Mankato, Minnesota

Pebble Books are published by Capstone Press
1710 Roe Crest Drive, North Mankato, Minnesota, 56003.
www.capstonepub.com

Printed in the United States of America in North Mankato, Minnesota.
032013   007253R

Library of Congress Cataloging-in-Publication Data
Frost, Helen, 1949–
    We need auto mechanics / by Helen Frost.
    p. cm.—(Helpers in our community)
    Includes bibliographical references and index.
    ISBN-10: 0-7368-2574-6 (hardcover)
    ISBN-13: 978-0-7368-2574-0 (hardcover)
    1. Automobiles—Maintenance and repair—Vocational guidance—Juvenile
literature. 2. Automobile mechanics—Juvenile literature. [1. Automobile mechanics.
2. Automobiles—Maintenance and repair. 3. Occupations.] I. Title. II. Series.
TL152.F76 2005
629.28′72′023—dc22   2003024186

Summary: Simple text and photographs describe and illustrate auto mechanics.

Note to Parents and Teachers

The Helpers in Our Community series supports national social
studies standards for units related to community helpers and their
roles. This book describes and illustrates auto mechanics. The
photographs support early readers in understanding the text. This
book also introduces early readers to subject-specific vocabulary
words, which are defined in the Glossary. Early readers may need
assistance to read some words and to use the Table of Contents,
Glossary, Read More, Internet Sites, and Index/Word List sections
of the book.

Table of Contents

4

Auto Mechanics

Auto mechanics work on cars. They help cars run well.

Auto mechanics check the oil in cars. They also fix engines.

Auto mechanics
change tires.

Auto mechanics
check and fix brakes.

Auto mechanics take out old car parts. They put in new car parts.

Tools They Use

Auto mechanics use wrenches to tighten and loosen nuts.

Auto mechanics use lifts to raise cars into the air.

Auto mechanics use computers to check car parts.

Car Safety

Auto mechanics help keep cars safe to drive.

Glossary

brake—a part that slows down or stops a vehicle

engine—a machine that changes an energy source, such as gasoline, into movement

mechanic—someone who is skilled at operating or repairing machinery; auto mechanics work on cars.

nut—a small metal piece that holds a car part in place

oil—a thick greasy liquid that burns easily and does not mix with water; motor oil is used to make machines run smoothly.

wrench—a tool with grips that tightens and loosens nuts

Read More

Miller, Heather. *Cars.* Wheels, Wings, and Water. Chicago: Heinemann Library, 2003.

Winne, Joanne. *A Day with a Mechanic.* Hard Work. New York: Children's Press, 2001.

Internet Sites

FactHound offers a safe, fun way to find Internet sites related to this book. All of the sites on FactHound have been researched by our staff.

Here's how:

1. Visit *www.facthound.com*
2. Type in this special code **0736825746** for age-appropriate sites. Or enter a search word related to this book for a more general search.
3. Click on the **Fetch It** button.

FactHound will fetch the best sites for you!

Index/Word List

air, 17
brakes, 11
cars, 5, 7, 13, 17,
  19, 21
change, 9
check, 7, 11, 19
computers, 19
engines, 7

fix, 7, 11
nuts, 15
oil, 7
run, 5
safe, 21
tires, 9
work, 5
wrenches, 15

Word Count: 79
Early-Intervention Level: 12

Editorial Credits

Mari C. Schuh, editor; Abby Bradford, Bradford Design Inc., cover designer;
  Enoch Peterson, book designer; Wanda Winch, photo researcher; Karen Hieb,
  product planning editor

The author thanks the children's library staff at the Allen County Public Library in
Fort Wayne, Indiana, for research assistance.